A Better Way: Making Better Choices

RICKY THOMAS GORDON

Gordon, R.T. A Better Way: Making Better Choices.

This book is available at amazon.com

Kindle ASIN: B00HSWMQAK
Paperback ISBN: 1494970767
Paperback ISBN-13: 978-1494970765

A Better Way: Making Better Choices
Author: Ricky Thomas Gordon
Publication: 2014

Acknowledgements
Cover and interior: Romel R. Saplaco, Byromedia Computer Consulting, www.byromedia.com

Photo Credit: road sign, edward musiak, edwardmusiak, http://www.flickr.com/photos/edwardmusiak/8394425334/, Creative Commons Attribution 2.0 Generic (CC BY 2.0), http://creativecommons.org/licenses/by/2.0/

Dedication

I have interacted with so many people in my life and each one has affected me in some way. I want to recognize some of those who have had the most impact on my life. All personal relationships require us to make choices. I have been encouraged most to make positive, constructive choices by my wife of forty years. Sarah has been my most constant exhorter to choose a better way—God's way. Having ten children, three sons-in-law and one daughter-in-law plus four grandchildren only increases the daily requirements to make good choices. So, I say thank you to Sarah; Chris & Chihiro; Ando, Catherine, Isaac, Andreas, & Ryan; Sonny & Elizabeth; Akihiro, Micah, & Lia Joy; Ericah, Jason, Matthew, Hannah, Matison, and Aya. Adding to this mix are Ako, who has lived and worked with us for the past twenty-five years, and her daughter, Emma. We've averaged seventeen people living in our house for the past five years. At times we've kept eight foster infants and toddlers, several of whom I owe a special debt of gratitude for the lessons they've taught me. These include Shota, Ma-kun, and Rin.

My extended family includes all the brothers and sisters of Living Way Church in Shizuoka. We've had several hundred pass through our church and lives over the past 26 years. Each one has contributed something to my life and, thus, to this book.

So I dedicate *A Better Way* to my two families. Thank you for allowing me to be a part of your lives. Thank you for providing so many opportunities to make good choices. Please forgive me for the times I did not make the better choice.

Table of Contents

Preface

The life we are now living is the sum total of the thousands upon thousands of choices we have made. In every situation we must choose. Too many times we look back, sometimes many years later, and realize we could have made a better choice. We could have chosen a Better Way. Whether we are faced with only two alternatives or a seemingly endless array of choices, our innate desire is to make the best choice possible to insure both our current and future happiness.

Speaking at the Fellowship Foundation National Prayer Breakfast in Washington, D.C. on February 7, 2013, Dr. Benjamin Carson, the director of the Pediatric Neurosurgery Division at Johns Hopkins Hospital, said his mother would never accept any excuses from her children. She would ask, "Do you have a brain?" When they would answer, "Yes," she would respond, "Then you could have thought your way out of it." She didn't allow them to blame their friends or their circumstances for decisions they made. She encouraged them to think about their choices and learn to make better decisions.

It is my hope that through the following strategies I am presenting we will all learn to think and make better choices. Don't make excuses. Don't blame others. There is almost always a Better Way. Better choices lead to better results.

The choices presented here were originally written over a three year period and included in newsletters sent to friends and supporters. They were titled "Coping Strategies." Each one was based on events that happened in our family and how we learned to cope with often unexplained changes. The best definition of coping I found and used is, "To cope is to face and deal with responsibilities, problems, or difficulties, especially successfully or in a calm or adequate manner."[1]

Unless otherwise indicated, all scripture quotations are taken from the New American Standard Version of the Bible.

Except for the names of family members and a few close friends, I have not used the real names of people when describing events and situations.

Notes

[1] Dictionary.com Dictionary & Thesaurus, LLC, iTouch application

A Better Way:
Making Better Choices

Better Way 1: See The Individual

The noise is deafening at times. The activity on the floor is constant and doesn't end until almost midnight then starts again by seven or eight. Two newborns adapting to life without the touch and voice of the mother they experienced inside the womb. Te-chan is on life support. Eight children in foster care, five of them born with Down Syndrome. Overwhelming is not an adequate word. None of my former coping skills are adequate for this situation. Paul said, "...momentary light affliction is producing for us an eternal weight of glory far beyond all comparison, while we look not at the things which are seen, but at the things which are not seen..."[1] But, with Hitomu drooling on me as he tries to crawl up my leg while I am feeding Rin in her high chair and Shota screaming because Ma-kun pushed him over, it is almost impossible to see the unseen. How do I handle the "seen" when it's in constant, demanding motion?

"See" each as an individual. No one spontaneously breaks into dance like Shota. Tomoki is alive to each and every experience and gives unrestrained vent to any and all emotions. When Ma-kun jumps from the coffee table into your arms, he throws his head back, looks heavenward, and leaps without ever doubting someone will catch him. And, Rin... while she is wary of strangers, delights in the appearance of "daddy."

1

Last night as she sat on my lap facing me, I interrupted one of her favorite activities, bouncing her head off my stomach, when I broke into song. She stared, almost blank faced, as I sang an old scripture song to her. When I finished, without changing her blank stare, she started clapping. That was priceless.

When I told Elizabeth, my second daughter, I was learning to look at the individual instead of the group, she commented, "God doesn't look at YOU as a group! He looks at you as one person." Jesus said, "Verily I say unto you, inasmuch as ye have done it unto ONE of the LEAST of these my brethren, ye have done it unto me."[2] I'm learning to do it unto ONE at a time and see ONE at a time. Now, if I can just teach the babies to scream, need a diaper change, and get a bottle one-at-a-time.

More

"So do not worry about tomorrow; for tomorrow will care for itself. Each day has enough trouble of its own."[3] If I said that, someone would accuse me of having a pessimistic attitude, but this was the Master, the Lord of Creation, speaking. Jesus was trying to teach us to live in the now. Deal with the issues—and the people—at hand. Take care of the troubles of today and don't worry about those in the future.

I heard Bro. A.S. Worley once teach about Hebrews 11:1 in which he emphasized the first word— now.

He said "Now faith is..." Faith must be exercised in the "now," in the "present." You may not make it to the future if you don't exercise faith in the "now." Only God can see and live in the past, present, and future because He is outside our time domain. We only have the "now."

By seeing the individual, by focusing on the problem that I am facing right now, I will reduce my stress. We compound the pressure we feel right now by adding our worries about tomorrow and next week and next year.

Rin only needs one diaper changed at a time. She may need five diapers a day but I only need to deal with one right now. If I think about 5 diapers a day, 35 a week, 1,825 a year for perhaps 3 years which will be 5,475 diapers, then I feel I just can't do it. If I really want to get distressed, think of the 8 babies and that will be 14,600 diapers that will need changing this year! Not only do we need a new landfill just for my household but I want to jump off the roof!

I don't need to compound my stress with such thoughts. I just need to see this one little individual who has an overflowing nappy right now. Change this one diaper and she will play contently for a few more hours. I can do that. One baby at a time—one diaper at a time. And you know what? It doesn't take that much faith to change one diaper at a time. I don't yet have the faith for 14,600 changes. BUT, I don't need that kind of faith.

I can reduce my stress by seeing the individual and by concentrating on one problem and one task at a time. Live in the now and exercise my faith for right now. The Better Way is to see the individual at hand.

Notes

[1] 2 Corinthians 4:17-18
[2] Matthew 25:40 KJV
[3] Matthew 6:34

Better Way 2: Give Tangible Thanks

Rushing out the door with a cup of coffee I spill precious ounces of caffeine down the stairs and onto my pants. I step in dog poo the kids didn't clean up from the darling beagle I never wanted but they all swore they would care for if I'd only buy her. Sitting my cup on the dash I look up from starting the engine to see that the birds my wife so dearly appreciates for raising their young every summer in our garage have anointed my windshield with their excreted offerings. My pants are stained, the car smells like doggie do, I can't see out the windshield, and I'm late again for class.

The scriptures tell us to give thanks "in" every situation[1] and "for" every situation[2] and do it with a grateful heart. We can always give thanks that Jesus died for our sins; our sins are forgiven; we have entered into eternal life from the moment we are born again; we have abundant life; and, I could go on and on. However, those benefits and blessings don't seem very real when you are exhausted, constantly not doing what you want to do because of the demands of others, and animals (both domesticated and wild) seem to have joined a conspiracy to get you. So, how do I give thanks and how does this spiritual imperative change my attitude in the here and now?

Babies crying, siblings at war, bills to pay, unsatisfied mates, and unrepentant creatures are all way, too, real. So, make your thanks real, tangible. I really like this word, "tangible." It means "able to be touched or perceived through the sense of touch; capable of being understood and evaluated, and therefore regarded as real."[3] Too often the spiritual blessings noted in paragraph two, are not really "capable of being understood" at a visceral level and therefore don't always relieve stress when I give thanks for them. When you are at the survival level, you don't philosophize very well. When your stress inducers are all too tangible, start your thanks at that level!

My "tangible thanks" include:

"Thank you Lord, I don't come home to an empty house."

"Thank you Lord, I don't have any more car payments. It may not be a Ferrari but it works and it's mine."

"Thank you Lord, I have food and I don't have to worry about breakfast tomorrow morning."

"Thank You people care enough about my ability or wisdom or approval to interrupt me—again and again and again..."

"After reading Spurgeon's *Eccentric Preachers*, I thank you Lord I was born in 1952 and not 1852!"

"Lord, thank you for opening my eyes to see that I am truly blessed with REAL, Tangible people and things!"

More

I am blessed in every situation. No matter how bad the circumstances or how unfairly I am being treated, there is always a blessing. In the movie, *Fiddler on the Roof*, the wise and comical rabbi of the community tells his people, "There is a blessing for everything." One of the villagers asks, "Is there a blessing for the czar?" Thinking for only a moment, he replies, "Yes. May the Lord bless and keep the czar, (pregnant pause)... far, far from us!" At this point in the movie, although they are poor, they are blessed because they are too far removed from the seat of power to be harassed by the czar and the political upheaval that is coming.

Open my eyes, Lord, to see Your blessings I do not see. Point out the special acts of kindness You have showered upon me that I have not recognized.

I have just shared with my freshmen English students the story of the first Thanksgiving. As part of this story I tell how God prepared Squanto to be a special blessing to the Pilgrims. If you were schooled, like me, in the period where we did not even mention the native Americans contribution to Thanksgiving, you probably don't know much about Squanto.

The Pilgrims arrived at Plymouth Rock in November of 1620. They probably met Squanto in the spring of 1621 and were shocked to hear him speak clear, British English. He not only taught them how to survive in the new land but became their interpreter and negotiator with Chief Massasoit and the other local Indians. The head of the colony wrote later that Squanto was "a special instrument of God for their good, beyond their expectation."[4] God's preparation of this "special instrument" began 16 years before.

In 1605 Squanto and four other Indians were captured and taken to England to learn English and provide information about the best places to establish trading posts and colonies. After 9 years in England, he was transported back to America by Capt. John Smith [of Pocahontas' fame] arriving in Plymouth in 1614. Shortly after returning home he was captured by the notorious Capt. Thomas Hunt, taken to Spain, and sold as a slave. He was bought by a group of friars opposed to slavery, introduced to Christianity, and set free. After 4 years in Spain he was able to return to England and eventually journeyed back to New England. He arrived 6 months before the Pilgrims.

To his horror he learned that "not a man, woman, or child of his own tribe was left alive! During the previous four years, a mysterious plague had broken out among them, killing every last one. So complete was the devastation that the neighboring tribes had shunned the area ever since. The Pilgrims had settled in a cleared area that belonged to no one. Their nearest neighbors, the Wampanoags, were about 50 miles to the southwest. Stripped of his identity and his reason for living, Squanto wandered aimlessly until he joined the Wampanoags, having nowhere else to go."[5] It was Samoset, a chief of the Algonquins visiting the area, who introduced him to the Pilgrims.

When Squanto was captured and taken to England in 1605 I'm sure he did not see that as a blessing. Yet, he got a chance to begin afresh when Capt. John Smith took him home. He must have been greatly discouraged during that long voyage to Spain as a slave. Bought and set free, he had another chance to start over. For 4 years in Spain he must have wondered why he had to be separated from his family, friends, and culture. Only after he met the Pilgrims did he come to understand why God had saved his life by letting him be in Spain. He had been prepared in England by learning not only English but the ways of the British and spared the agony and suffering of dying with his tribe.

He was only with the Pilgrims for a little over a year before his own death in 1622. Yet in that one year he helped insure the successful establishment of the Plymouth colony and the eventual founding of the United States of America. He is still remembered today and was truly a "special instrument of God."

Knowing he was close to death Squanto told William Bradford, the second governor of the Plymouth Colony, that he wanted to go to the white man's heaven, not the Indian's, and made a clear profession of faith in Jesus Christ.

Give thanks for the blessings you know and understand now. Like King David, pray, "Lord, 'give me understanding that I may live.'"[6] Later, you can give tangible thanks for all those blessings that were disguised as troubles and tragedies earlier in your life.

Notes

[1] 1 Thessalonians 5:18
[2] Ephesians 5:20
[3] Dictionary.com Dictionary & Thesaurus, LLC, iTouch application
[4] Chuck Missler, The First Thanksgiving
[5] *Ibid.*
[6] Psalms 119:144

Better Way 3: Let God Define Normal

"...being normal isn't necessarily a virtue. It rather denotes a lack of courage."[1]

"Dad, are we normal?" Jason, my thoughtful 2nd son, asked a few months back.

"No, Jason. We're not normal in America or Japan. Normal people don't have ten children and live in a foreign country."

These days, I could add a lot more reasons to that answer. For instance, January 3, 2010, the first Sunday of the year, Sarah and Micah (daughter number three) stayed home with two sick babies and they kept a few more so the rest of the family could go to church without too much strain. We just happened to have friends visiting from Australia who were coming to lunch after church. Sarah and Micah thought they would also have a little extra time to prepare the meal.

A few minutes into my New Year's message, I saw Elizabeth jump up in a panic and run out the front door. Ericah ran out the side door. It was only after the rest of us arrived home we learned what happened. The following story is as accurate as I can piece it together.

Micah was kneeling on the floor changing one of the babies who had deposited a massive BM in his diaper. Ma-kun crawled over, grabbed a handful of the solid waste, and started sampling and redistributing the dark matter. Sarah picked him up and headed for the shower. In the mean time, Shota, who loves popcorn, started stuffing his mouth as fast as he could. Choking on the kernels, he began throwing up beside Micah and the baby. Micah, in her not so delicate way, yelled for her mother. Sarah came flying out of the bath area, tripped on something [she still doesn't remember what happened], and landed face down in the living room. That's when Micah called the church and frantically requested immediate backup.

Sometimes my life is so far beyond what I see in others, beyond how I grew up, and even beyond what it was a year ago, I almost scream, "Lord, I just want to be normal." But, immediately, I know the problem with that cry: "Who defines what is normal?" When Paul wrote the Corinthians, "Let all things be done decently and in order"[2] he was not giving us license to define what is "decent" and what is "in order." We have used that verse in every generation to define what is acceptable in a meeting and even what is an acceptable way to preach and teach. I am convinced that only the Holy Spirit can accurately define what is "decent and in order" in any and all situations. AND, only HE knows what is "normal" for "me" at any given point in time. You can relieve a lot of stress by letting HIM determine what is normal.

In my Oral Communication class at the university I asked a young girl on my left, "Are you a normal Japanese girl?" "Yes," came the immediate reply. I turned to a young girl on my right and asked the same question. "Of course," she said confidently. The student to my left, who had very limited English skills, was wearing black and gray clothes, no make-up, and black-rimmed glasses. The girl to my right had short cropped hair which she dyed a different color every week, played drums in a punk rock band on weekends, and spoke very fluent English. Looking at one and then the other, I asked, "How can both of you be normal?" I couldn't shake them. Each was convinced she was the typical Japanese girl. It is very important here to be considered "normal." A Japanese proverb says, "The nail that stands up gets hammered down."

> *"To be normal is the ideal aim of the unsuccessful."*[3]

Notes

[1] http://thinkexist.com/quotation/when_will_you_understand_ that_being_normal_isn-t/339676.html
[2] 1 Corinthians 14:40 (KJV)
[3] Carl Gustav Jung,
http://thinkexist.com/quotes/carl_gustav_jug

Better Way 4: Don't Get Angry, Get Your Camera.

I open the door, step inside, and look up the 18 steps leading to our second floor. At odd angles and different positions, on almost every step, are shoes of various colors, shapes, and sizes—no two matching. The boys have been enjoying their favorite game! By the boys, I mean Shota and Ma-kun, both three and a half years old Down Syndrome kids. We have a gate at the top of the steep stairs to prevent them from tumbling down. So, they love to take the shoes arranged neatly in rows at the top of the second floor entrance and throw them through or under the bars of the gate as far down the stairs as possible. They've done a particularly outstanding job today. Instead of getting angry, I go for my camera. We've never had any children do this before!

Better Way 4 is, "Don't get angry, get your camera!" How many times do we explode and obsess over an event but later laugh as we tell friends and family about the disaster that is now a treasured memory. I wish I had learned this when I first had children, not now, thirty-three years later!

When Jason was three and Matthew two, we were keeping a small boy, about one and a half, while he awaited moving to his adoptive family. All the ladies of the house left Chris (who was 17 at the time) and me to babysit. I got distracted doing something in my office area and assumed that Chris was watching the three boys. I suddenly realized I didn't hear anything. Silence is NOT golden in such circumstances.

I rushed into the living room and didn't see anyone. Then I heard joyful laughter in the corner of the kitchen. [For those of you who don't have children or it has been too long for you to remember, "joyful laughter" may or may NOT mean all is well.] Rounding the corner I found the source of all the "joy." Jason was holding a plastic honey bear over the heads of the other two boys squeezing the remaining honey on to their hair and all over their bodies. Matthew and Matti were gleefully slapping their hands in the honey on the floor. They were covered in the sticky, sweet fluid.

My first thought was not, "Where's my camera?" but rather, "Sarah's gonna kill me." My second thought was, "Where's Chris?" Then I heard him pounding on the metal door that blocked off our staircase from the first floor. It seems he had stepped out for a moment and Jason had locked the door behind him. Because I was in my study, I couldn't hear his pounding on the metal door.

Unfortunately, in our panic and fear of the women returning, Chris and I cleaned up the boys and the kitchen before we thought about taking a picture. Gone forever is that prize winning photograph.

More

"...everyone must be quick to hear [a ready listener*], slow to speak, and slow to anger; for the anger of man does not achieve the righteousness of God."[1]

James is encouraging us to slow down the process. Take the time to listen before speaking or getting angry. Proverbs tells us that "Spouting off before listening to the facts is both shameful and foolish."[2] The Message translates this as "Answering before listening is both stupid and rude." Do something to slow down your reaction.

Dr. Rhinehart, one of my professors at Auburn University, taught most of his classes on the first floor of Haley Center. His office was on the ninth floor. Every day he would eschew the elevator in favor of the stairs. Whenever he had a disgruntled student who wanted to angrily protest a grade, Dr. Rhinehart would say, "Let's talk about this in my office," and lead the student to the stairs. By the time they reached the ninth floor, the anger and the wind were gone from the student. Dr. Rhinehart was fine but most students were unable to proceed with much force. He not only delayed their reaction but gave them a physical outlet for their emotion.

An American teacher I know married a local Japanese man. Before she became fluent in Japanese they had to argue using dictionaries. By the time they had looked up the names they wanted to call each other in the dictionary, most of the steam was gone from their arguments. They frequently ended in laughter because they couldn't find the words they wanted fast enough.

Slow down your reaction. Defuse your anger. If it means walking up nine flights of stairs or 18 steps and searching for your camera in the jumble of your bedroom, let those moments calm you down. It's better to have a photo to remember than a memory to regret.

Bishop Joseph Garlington says he and his wife live by a maxim, "If it's going to be funny later, it's funny now."[3] Learn to see the humor now, not just later. It is also great to have a picture to go with your story!

Notes

[1] James 1:19-20 (*The Amplified Bible includes "[a ready listener]")
[2] Proverbs 18:13 NLT
[3] Bishop Joseph Garlington, speaking at Bethel Church, Redding, CA, 3/3/13

Better Way 5: Make Healthy Comparisons

In 2007 I attended an international church conference in Berne, Switzerland. The pastor of the hosting church had visited Japan several times and knew my family and ministry. To save money and to build relationships we stayed with members of the local congregation. The Swiss pastor intentionally placed me with a particular family in his church. He said, "These people are struggling with their situation. They are discouraged. I think you can help them." That's all he told me. I had no idea what they needed.

The second day I had time to relax and talk over coffee with the host husband and wife. They asked me a few questions about my life in Japan. I simply talked about what we do every day with all the babies and children. I didn't say anything spiritual. I just described our routine and a few of the problems we've faced. They were friendly and seemed genuinely interested so I talked without reservation. After about an hour, the husband leaned back and said, "I feel a lot better now. Compared to you we really don't have a very stressful life. Your situation is much worse than ours!" That wasn't particularly encouraging to me but he and his wife felt relieved and built up! Later, my pastor friend thanked me for encouraging his church members. "I knew you could help them," he said.

I know we can get discouraged by comparing ourselves with others and that sometimes we can even excuse our own sins because they don't seem as bad as someone else's, but I do believe there are comparisons that can encourage and strengthen us. After reading about the persecution and suffering of some famous pastors like Charles Spurgeon, Jonathan Edwards, Charles Simeon, and others, I realize I haven't suffered at all compared to them. I've been very blessed and protected. Compared to Heidi Baker, a thirty-year missionary in Mozambique who's responsible for feeding 10,000 children a day, cooking for the 20 people who eat at our house daily isn't such a big deal.

I'm also strengthened in my faith by realizing that if God can do that for them, He will do the same for me. I, therefore, believe there are healthy comparisons that can alleviate or dissipate some or all of the stress we may be experiencing. Better Way 5 is "Make Healthy Comparisons."

More

Half way through our 10 days mission trip to Indonesia, April 8, 2012, we were preparing to leave the city of Balikpapan on the island of Kalimantan when I realized my little bag was missing. The night before we had driven for an hour, rented a speedboat, and crossed the bay to visit a church on the other side of a peninsula. Then the pastor drove us for another hour to reach a church he was pioneering deep inside a rubber tree plantation.

After the meeting we made the return trip. Somewhere on the way home my very important little Eagle Creek travel bag disappeared. We searched the car, our hotel room, and even called the driver of the boat. As we headed for the airport to fly back to Jakarta I had to concede that my bag was gone. Inside that bag were my Japanese Alien Registration Card; Japanese driver's license; two credit cards; my university I.D.; my iPod with all my Bible programs, podcasts, e-books, and audio books; my Nokia cell phone; and my sunglasses.

My son-in-law was amazed that I wasn't more upset about the loss. A friend wrote later after I had written about this on Facebook, "I wish I could roll with the punches like you and not get so upset." Just a few years ago I would have been far more irritable and even complained to the Lord about such an attack while doing *His* business. Yes, this caused a lot of trouble. We had to quickly file a report with the local police before boarding our plane back to Jakarta so that I would have a police document to prove to Japanese immigration I had indeed lost my A.R. and to show the local police when I applied to replace my driver's license. And, I had to make numerous telephone calls in Indonesia and to Japan and America to cancel my credit cards and apply for replacement cards. We also had to quickly ascertain our financial situation since we no longer had any credit cards and must use cash for the next 5 days. So why wasn't I more stressed?

When I thought about the missing contents of my little bag and compared that to events that had just happened back in Shizuoka (Japan), my loss and inconvenience were just that—lost items that could be replaced and a momentary inconvenience. The day before my loss I learned a lady in our church had just lost her father to a terminal illness. The night I lost my bag, Sarah called to tell us that a young woman we had known for years had swallowed a massive dose of muscle relaxers and had left behind two small boys and a husband. The young woman's mother had just buried her own sister three months prior after watching her slowly succumb to a debilitating disease. My wife and four children were working night and day to care for the eight foster children in our home—two who were on respirators.

Compared to what others were facing, my loss was absolutely nothing. We were far from home but we were all safe, healthy, and well fed (although Hannah and I did have a hard time eating the frog soup). Every time I was tempted to complain to the Lord about my loss, I could just let it go and not waste my time and energy on such trivia. AND, let me report that God indeed took care of our cash flow issues. To our amazement, the very next church we visited paid all our hotel bills and gave us a nice offering. For a poor church they gave beyond their means and exceeded all the others before them. The pastor told Ando, "As a church we need to learn how to give." He had no idea how much he blessed us.

Comparisons can be healthy when they make us realize that our situation may be quite petty compared to others. Losing objects that can be replaced is nothing compared to losing people. What I may consider stress is not stress at all—it's just a minor inconvenience. Let it go and realize how blessed you really are.

Better Way 6: Recognize Personal Signs of Encouragement

When I learned I was being retired from Tokoha University after 16 years full time, I rode the emotional roller coaster as I contemplated my financial future. At times my confident faith that God would provide all we needed would take me to the high places but then there were moments when the overwhelming responsibilities of a husband and father sent me plummeting to new lows. The time before and immediately after my change was very stressful for me *AND* everyone associated with me. But, we serve a personal God who intervenes in ways only *we* can appreciate.

As a teacher, writer, and pastor I seem to always be in need of certain office supplies. For many years it seemed like I never had a paperclip when I needed it most. One day at *KenDai* (University of Shizuoka), I was rummaging through my briefcase looking for a paperclip hidden in some compartment or under papers but not finding one. Pushing my chair back from the desk, I noticed a shiny silver object on the floor. To my delight there were 3 paperclips between the desk and the platform where my rolling chair sat. I was like a small child finding a long lost treasured toy.

Holding the three clips in my hand, I heard the still, small voice of the Holy Spirit say, "I will provide all you need when you need it." Since that time, I have found paperclips in amazing places and every time I find one, I remember, "I will provide." Even as I crossed the classroom in my portable building to write this I found a beautiful lavender paperclip I had not noticed during the first 2 hours of class!

God gave Noah (and all future generations) rainbows, Gideon fleeces, and me paperclips. I know He wants to encourage each of us in a way especially designed to speak to *our* hearts. May the Holy Spirit open your eyes to see and recognize his personal signs of encouragement for you. Better Way 6 is recognize and be encouraged by God's personal signs of encouragement.

"When you see... you say... and it turns out that way."[1]

Notes

[1] Luke 12:54-56

Better Way 7: Let the Holy Spirit Apply The Word to Your Situation

Recently while attending a celebration, the Holy Spirit spoke a verse to me. As we were waiting to partake of the sumptuous buffet, I heard, "Thou preparest a table before me in the presence of mine enemies."[1] [The Holy Spirit often speaks to me in King James English because that is how I memorized most of the scriptures I know.] Immediately I understood some of the meaning but did not get the full understanding until the next day when I was sitting in a dentist's chair awaiting a root canal. It is amazing how close I can get to God when facing fear and pain or the fear of pain.

Although the event was a joyful one, our attendance represented a stressful situation for many—including my family. We knew we would see some people who had left our church with unresolved conflicts. The meaning of the Hebrew word for "enemies," *tsarar*, is "someone who show's hostility toward; someone who stirs up trouble, torments, or causes distress."[2] That pretty accurately describes several of the people who were at the event.

So, this was my time to experience Psalms 23:5. The food was wonderful, and except for a few tense moments, the celebration was very enjoyable.

At the dentist's office, I gained two important insights into our experience. One, when God prepares a table, even in the presence of your enemies, He goes above and beyond what we could hope or ask. About thirty years ago, before I ever dreamed of moving to Japan, a friend took a business trip to Tokyo. When he returned he told me his hosts had taken him to a Kobe Beef restaurant. He said, "Kobe beef is the best in the world. If you ever go to Japan, you must get someone to take you to eat Kobe beef!" Well, I visited Japan 2 times before moving and had lived here for over 25 years but had never had Kobe beef until that night! I had no idea how good it was until then. Once I found the steak in the buffet, I went back three times during the evening. One of my children exclaimed to me later, "Dad, did you know that steak cost $45 a pound (¥8,000/kg)?!" My first taste of Kobe beef was at the "table prepared for me in the presence of mine enemies." God is so good!

My second insight came when I remembered the rest of the verse, "...Thou anointest my head with oil, my cup runneth over." I felt the Lord say that since He had fulfilled the first half of the verse, I should pray and believe for the second half to be fulfilled. I am convinced that if God prepares a table with Kobe beef for me in the presence of those who show hostility toward my wife and I, then He will certainly pour out an anointing that overflows!

It is much easier to persevere through a situation and to revisit the memory, no matter how painful, when we let the Holy Spirit apply the Word. Better Way 7: Let the Holy Spirit Apply The Word to Your Situation.

"...how good is a timely word!"[3]

Notes

[1] Psalms 23:5 KJV
[2] Enhanced Strong's Dictionary, New American Standard Bible, Olive Tree Bible Software, Inc., Version 5.5.10, 2013.
[3] Proverbs 15:23 NIV

Better Way 8: Wait for God's Interpretation

Stress increases when we can't understand what's happening or why? If I can't see any useful purpose in my circumstances, why should I persevere? Why shouldn't I just quit? Why not just walk out and disappear into the increasing homeless population or jump from the tallest building and end it all? In the midst of his struggles, David cried out to God "...give me understanding that I may live."[1]

In his hymn, "God Moves in a Mysterious Way," William Cowper wrote:

God moves in a mysterious way
His wonders to perform;
He plants his footsteps in the sea,
And rides upon the storm. [v. 1]

His purposes will ripen fast,
Unfolding every hour;
The bud may have a bitter taste,
But sweet will be the flower. [v. 5]

Blind unbelief is sure to err,
And scan his work in vain:
God is his own interpreter,
And He will make it plain. [v. 6]

When Moses was instructed to create the bronze serpent, put it on a pole, and tell the people that whoever looked on the serpent would not die, no one, including Moses, understood the significance of his action.[2] The scripture does not give any clarification and the Holy Spirit does not explain the symbolism for 1,500 years! It is only when Jesus says, ""As Moses lifted up the serpent in the wilderness, even so must the Son of Man be lifted up; so that whoever believes will in Him have eternal life"[3] that we get the explanation.

My last three years in America before becoming a missionary in Japan were the most difficult years of my life (up until that time). We weren't in poverty. We weren't suffering from any debilitating diseases. We were intensely involved with people grappling with their personal issues—both past and present. My wife and I became the target (the reason, the excuse) for some dear saints' attempts to understand their past and explain their present. There were times I cried out like Jerry Clower's man, John, in the top of the tree fighting a cornered possum, which turned out to be a lynx. He was being so clawed up by the critter he shouted to his friend with the gun, "Just shoot up in heah amongst us cause one of us has got to have some relief!"[4]

Now, looking back 28 years (not 1,500), I can see that everything we endured was preparation for the mission field. No seminary or mission's training program could have anticipated or prepared us for what was to follow. When I can't understand what's happening and don't see any reason why, I need to see from God's perspective. That is possible because we are seated in the heavens and hidden with Christ in God.[5] Until I do see from His perspective, I need to keep trusting that God knows; God cares; and, He is working all things together for my good and His eternal purpose. I can have confidence that "God is His own interpreter, and He will make it plain." Wait for His interpretation.

Notes

[1] Psalms 119:144
[2] Numbers 21:8-9
[3] John 3:14-15
[4] Jerry Clower, *A Coon Huntin' Story (Knock Him Out John)*
[5] Colossians 3:3

Better Way 9: Believe You Are Far More Valuable Than You Know!

Around the first of the year there was a photograph of a giant tuna in the newspaper. When this tuna was swimming off the coast of Hokkaido, minding his own business, he had no idea he was so valuable. He was the first blue fin tuna to be auctioned off in the 2012 season. In the water he was just another big fish (269 kg/592 lb.) but when the bidding was done he sold for ¥56.49 million ($715,000!).[1]

Unending conflicts and perpetual problems can have such a debilitating effect that we lose sight of our personal worth. We may even feel we have no value to God or any one else. Day after day we faithfully keep doing the same old things, struggling to survive; but, for what purpose, for what benefit, even for whom do we keep going.

Paul understood these feelings when he wrote, "we are afflicted in every way, but not crushed; perplexed, but not despairing; persecuted, but not forsaken; struck down, but not destroyed."[2] At times he must have felt his problems and persecutions were never ending. Instead of going from strength to strength and faith to faith he was caught in a downward spiral of physical and emotional pain. "For we who live are constantly being delivered over to death..."[3] Does that describe what you feel?

If we can identify with the pain, then let's also identify with the victory. "Therefore, we do not lose heart, though our outer man is decaying, yet our inner man is being renewed day by day."[4] "For our light, momentary affliction (this slight distress of the passing hour) is ever more and more abundantly preparing and producing and achieving for us an everlasting weight of glory [beyond all measure, excessively surpassing all comparisons and all calculations, a vast and transcendent glory and blessedness never to cease!]."[5]

All that you are going through is producing something in you and for you. These stressful, seemingly counterproductive, experiences are actually increasing your personal worth! You may be like that blue fin tuna—you have no idea how valuable you are until the final auction!

And, just for your information, that tuna was purchased by a sushi chain that will slice the meat up into thin, raw layers for individual servings. One of our church members, a fish auctioneer, told me one piece of this sushi could sell for ¥2,000/$24! Bon appétit and take heart! You are far more valuable than you know!

Notes

[1] The Yomiuri Shimbun, January 19, 2012

[2] 2 Corinthians 4:8-9

[3] 2 Corinthians 4:11

[4] 2 Corinthians 4:16

[5] 2 Corinthians 4:17 Amplified Bible

Better Way 10: Know, Believe, & Confess

Arriving home after my evening university class, I walked through our front door and glanced at Sarah's English class meeting on the first floor. Two doctors, a nurse, and a social worker from Shizuoka Children's Hospital were seated at the round table with Sarah. My first thought, seemingly out of nowhere, was, "Miki's dead." I didn't step in and greet the class, which I frequently do. I just stood in the hall a few minutes, composed myself, and went upstairs.

It had been almost four weeks since baby Miki died. Most people cannot comprehend how the death of a three-month-old foster baby can affect us so much. After all, she wasn't "our child, our flesh & blood." What they don't realize is that to provide care for babies given up for adoption, we must bond with them. If a baby bonds with another person soon after birth they will be able to bond with their adoptive family later. If they don't bond soon, they may never bond with any one [Attachment Disorder]. So, we open our home and hearts and welcome each baby or child into our lives. We were preparing for Miki to go to her new adoptive family but were not prepared for her sudden and still unexplained death.

So, how have we coped with this perplexing and lingering loss when there are no answers for "why?" Our lives changed unexpectedly on April 2 with Miki's death. We had already undergone unexpected change on March 11, 2011, with the earthquake and tsunami that devastated northern Japan and caused a nuclear meltdown. *We cope with unexpected change by putting our trust in that which does NOT change.*

No matter what has happened or will happen, God's character and His Word do not change. "I am the Lord God, I change not."[1] "Jesus Christ is the same yesterday and today and forever."[2] "The sum of Your Word is truth, and every one of Your righteous ordinances is everlasting."[3] "God is good,"[4] and "God is love"[5]—no matter what happens. "God is our refuge and strength, a very present help in trouble."[6] The best way to cope with the innumerable changes in life, even the most painful, is to know, believe, and confess the unchanging Word of God. When he was very elderly the apostle John, wrote, "We have come to know and have believed the love which God has for us. God is love..."[7]

May we all come to know not only in our minds but also through our personal experience and may we believe the great love that God has for us. Confessing the truth of His everlasting Word helps work it into our hearts and lives. Move forward by choosing the better way: Know, Believe, and Confess.

Notes

[1] Malachi 3:6 KJV
[2] Hebrews 13:8
[3] Psalms 119:160
[4] Mark 10:18, Acts 10:38
[5] 1 John 4:8
[6] Psalms 46:1
[7] 1 John 4:16

Better Way 11: Forget None of His Benefits

My current events have been rather discouraging as I watch friends falter, some physically and some spiritually; and, we all await answers to long term prayers. It is very difficult to be a positive, enthusiastic leader when it **seems** we gather in His name but He doesn't show up and we agree in prayer but He doesn't answer. We know we walk by faith and not by sight but we all want to see some signs in our physical realm of the spiritual reality we know is there. How do I get from my feelings, "My God, my God, why hast thou forsaken me?"[1] to spiritual reality, "I will not leave you as orphans[2]... I am with you always, even to the end of the age."[3]

First of all let's get doctrinally clear. When Jesus took all the sins of the world on Himself and became sin for us, he could cry "My God, my God, why has thou forsaken me?" Note this is the only time Jesus did not refer to God as "Father." Once Jesus cried, "It is finished,"[4] (literally, "it is paid in full") he made an end to us ever being cut off from God. He will not break His promise that He "will never leave us." So, no matter what I "feel," I am never forsaken by God. I may not see the signs of His Presence or the results I long for, but He is always near and He promises that if we "draw near to God, He will draw near to us."[5]

Now, how do I cope when I "feel" God is not here and I don't yet "see" His handiwork? Psalms 103:1-5 details several ways to cope with these problems. I want to focus on one in verse 2, "forget none of His benefits." Verses 3-5 list some of those benefits. He pardons all my iniquities, heals all my diseases, redeems my life from the pit, crowns me with lovingkindness and compassion, satisfies my years with good things, and renews my youth like the eagles. That's quite a list of benefits.

So, when you feel like you're in the pit and you can't seem to find or sense God, make your own personal list of His benefits in your life and the lives of those around you. I've been very encouraged by just reviewing the testimonies of people I know who have been healed or who were barren but later gave birth to two or three children (2 women I know). I even look at their pictures on Facebook sometimes! Remembering God's miraculous financial provision time after time renews my faith that He will provide now and later. I always delight to quote my grandfather Gordon ("D") who told me, "I've had six doctors tell me that I was going to die. I buried them all! When it's the Master's time for me to go, then I'll die." Telling these stories to my children not only encourages me but also passes on our family history of interaction with God. Forget none of His benefits!

More

A few weeks ago (February, 2013) our church was praying for two people lost on a hiking trail in the Southern Alps of Japan. The older couple was not rescued in time and perished in a storm. Their bodies were found about 50 meters apart. Apparently the husband had tried to find help but failed. Thinking about these events I recall hearing people say, "What a terrible thing to die alone!"

As I pondered the incident, I heard the small voice of the Spirit whisper, "You will never die alone. Even if there are no other people around, you are not alone. Jesus is there. The angels are there. You will never be alone." Although I do not plan to die any time soon, that was very comforting. As a believer, I will always know His presence and His comfort. I choose this better way to think! What a benefit to being His child!

Notes

[1] Matthew 27:46 KJV
[2] John 14:18
[3] Matthew 28:20
[4] John 19:30
[5] James 4:8

Better Way 12: Listen To God Speak Thru Others

Friday morning, July 1, 2011, I bowed my head as our guest speaker from Sweden, began to pray. As he prayed and Ako interpreted, I was having my own conversation with God. I told the Lord, "I feel like I'm in a long, dark train tunnel, but I believe there is light at the end of the tunnel." The next sentence to his prayer was, "Yes Lord, there is light at the end of the tunnel." I almost fell out of my seat. God instantly confirmed what I had prayed to reinforce my hope.

Three weeks later I shared this testimony at the beginning of my message to encourage people that God does know and care and that He speaks to us— often through others. I closed by reading from 1 Samuel 3:1-10. I emphasized that we need to have a heart like Samuel in order to better hear from the Lord. Samuel said, "Speak, Lord, for Your servant is listening."

After lunch, a church member whose work took him away from town often asked to speak with me. He said, "When you read those verses from 1 Samuel I started shaking all over. I knew God was speaking to me. Last Sunday I went to a church in Tokyo because I had to meet with the pastor about remodeling part of his building. He preached on the verses you closed with today." His meeting with the pastor had been a miraculous answer to prayer. He hadn't had a remodeling job in six months and was close to bankruptcy and despair. One of the lessons he had learned was that God knew and cared and did indeed speak to him through others.

Sometimes all we need to help us keep going is to hear from God. Peter said we could "cast all our cares upon Him, because He cares for us."[1] He shows us He cares by communicating his concern. In Hebrews 1:1 we are told that God spoke to us in the past through His prophets and then through His son Jesus. He continues to speak to us through His written Word, through the Holy Spirit, AND through other human beings.

After waiting for almost two years since I had felt God told me I could quit my job and go on the mission field without anyone else feeling that or confirming what I had heard, the Lord began to speak to me one night from Ezekiel 12. A few days later I went to hear a man speak at the local Holiday Inn in Decatur, AL. At the end of the meeting he began to prophesy over people. We were all standing but I kept my head bowed. Honestly, there were people in the audience who had left our church under less than amicable circumstances and I really didn't want them to see me.

"I have a word for you," the speaker said from up front. I didn't look up until the man beside me tapped me on the shoulder and said, "He's talking to you." When I looked up, the speaker looked me right in the eye, and said, "Yes, you. Come to the front please." I had no choice but to obey. Standing in front of everyone, I heard him quote word-for-word from the verses in Ezekiel 12 I had received a few nights earlier. The words I remember were, "Prepare to move. I am going to move you from this place to another." A close friend and trusted brother in the Lord, who was in the meeting, approached me before I left the room. "What's God been saying to you? I didn't like that word you got but I feel like it was from the Lord." That night was the confirmation that started our exit for the mission field.

God knows and cares AND He does still speak to His people. He often speaks through others to us. When you agree with Samuel by saying, "Speak, Lord, for Your servant is listening,"[2] don't just listen for a James Earl Jones' voice to boom out of heaven. Pay attention to what others say. Listen for His Voice through the voices of those around you.

More

On Monday night, September 26, 2011, at 8:30 P.M. my daughter Micah was driving Aya (our youngest) and Emma (Ako's daughter) to Yokohama to spend a few days with her. Micah's still not sure what happened. She knows she suddenly saw a van right beside her and must have swerved to keep from hitting it and crashed into the guardrail. Our ten year old Suzuki *Cultus* went into a spin, and at some point, hit the van. Both air bags deployed in the front seats. Emma was in the back but had not refastened her seatbelt after they had stopped for food. Although Micah suffered from whiplash for a few weeks, all three were miraculously unharmed. The policeman at the scene said he couldn't see how they escaped without injury. The *Cultus* wasn't so lucky. We had a year and a half left on the *shaken* (inspection sticker) but there was no repairing the car.

Sarah and Ako drove to the scene and brought the three girls back to our house. We were all shaken by the accident and the thought that it could have been so deadly. We were grateful for God's protection but I was disturbed it happened at all.

The next morning I was on my way to work listening to a teaching by Mark Virkler on *Hearing the Voice of God* when he said, "When I come to Him in prayer sometimes I'm all stressed out saying, 'God I'm dying!' He said, 'Be at peace. I'm here.' I said, 'You couldn't be here. Look at this WRECK!' He says, 'Mark, it's okay. It's all under control.'"[3] I knew God was speaking to me. Mark didn't have to say, "wreck." He could just as easily have said "mess," or "disaster," or "chaos." Instead, he said, "wreck." The Holy Spirit chose the word— several years before I listened to the CD. I listened to this part of the teaching again and again, letting those words sink into my soul. "Be at peace. I'm here. It's okay. It's all under control."

Notes

[1] 1 Peter 5:7 KJV
[2] 1 Samuel 3:9-10
[3] Mark Virkler, *Hearing the Voice of God*, CD 1, Track 7

Better Way 13: Don't Just Live For NOW

*"A good man leaves an inheritance to
his children's children..."*[1]

About a week after returning from their
honeymoon in Thailand, Akihiro and Micah visited
our family in Shizuoka and returned to their new
home in Yokohama with our 10 year old car full of
wedding presents. They needed to borrow our car
until they could find a replacement for Akihiro's
old car he had junked when he started his new job.
The following week Micah called me at three in the
afternoon. She had gone shopping at a very large
Nittori, a department store that sells many unique
household goods. Our old car wouldn't start. To
sum up her situation, she was living in a strange
city where she knew very few people; she had
almost no cash on her and no credit cards; she was
not a member of JAF (the Japanese equivalent of
AAA); her husband was unreachable at work; and,
Micah is totally non-mechanical. So, dear old dad
got a call.

I told her to go back inside and explain her dilemma
to the *Nittori* people. This store is actually sharing a
building with a very large electrical goods company
named Yamada Denki. Together they just happened
to be hosting an Auto Fair on the grounds that day.
Micah met an eager young man at the Auto Fair
who was excited to demonstrate one of their

products, a portable battery charger/starter. In just a few moments our old Suzuki was running again. [This was before the car was totaled as I shared in the previous chapter.] Micah drove to the nearest gas station and had the battery tested. The attendant asked, "Have you had any trouble with this before?" Micah told him this was the very first time, to which he replied, "That's hard to believe because this battery is so dead it doesn't even register on my meter." He said she could drive somewhere else to buy a battery but if the engine died on the way he was sure she couldn't restart it with this battery. Micah knew exactly how much cash she had in her purse when she asked him what he would charge. "¥7,000," he said. Micah asked, "Are you sure that is the total cost of the battery and installation because that is all the money I have in my purse." The man laughed and reassured her that was the TOTAL cost. Micah emptied her purse and drove home in a few minutes.

When she told me the story, I heard the Holy Spirit speak inside, "Your daughter is enjoying the benefits of all the years you and Sarah have sewn seeds of kindness and laid down your lives for others. The blessing is from generation to generation." The choices you make today will affect generations to come. Every time you choose to do the right thing; every time you swear to your own hurt and don't change; every time you choose to endure and suffer when you could escape, you are sewing seeds of blessing that will not only affect you but all those who follow after. Paul, who endured a great deal more than most of us ever will, wrote in Romans, "For I consider that the sufferings of this present time (this present life) are not worth being compared with the glory that is about to be revealed to us and in us and for us and conferred on us!"[2] That glory and blessing does not end with our demise but continues from generation to generation. So don't give up and don't drown in the "slough of despond (swamp of despair)."[3] You and I do not live just for NOW.

> *"...He is God, the faithful God, who keeps His covenant and His lovingkindness to a thousandth generation with those who love Him and keep His commandments."[4]*
> *"I'm establishing my covenant between me and you, a covenant that includes your descendants, a covenant that goes on and on and on, a covenant that commits me to be your God and the God of your descendants."[5]*

Notes

[1] Proverbs 13:20
[2] Romans 8:18 Amplified Bible
[3] John Bunyan, *Pilgrim's Progress*
[4] Deuteronomy 7:9
[5] Genesis 17:7 The Message

Better Way 14: You Are Having An Impact

"Cast your bread on the surface of the waters, for you will find it after many days."[1]

"This is Melody. Do you remember me?"

"I sure do. I recognized your voice."

"I was just on my way to the baptism of a young girl I led to the Lord and I remembered my own baptism and I just wanted to call. That short time I was in your church in Japan had a profound impact on my life. I just wanted you to know."

I hadn't heard from Melody since she returned to New Zealand eight or nine years earlier. She was only with us for about one month. She asked me to baptize her but balked when I said she needed to share a brief testimony before the baptism. Melody was so hesitant to share I began to doubt she had had a genuine salvation experience. Finally she agreed to let me interview her instead of standing alone in front of everyone. I don't remember much else about her. I just remember my impression of her as a party girl who didn't take life very seriously. When she left Japan I didn't think she would ever follow through on her commitment once she returned home.

"After I left Japan I became a missionary in a third world country. I met another missionary there, we got married, and now we are back in New Zealand for a while." She didn't talk long because she had to get to the water baptism. "I just wanted you and Sarah to know how much you influenced my life when I was with you."

I was absolutely shocked, blessed, and very emotional when I hung up. Now when I get discouraged because I have worked so hard to help someone, lead them in the ways of the Lord, and be a positive Christian example just to have them walk away, I try to remember that phone call. We really never know how we are impacting the lives of people—both intimate friends and casual acquaintances. We won't know this side of eternity. God is so gracious to let us get a glimpse now and then of the good ground that actually produced a crop from the seeds we had sewn.

Although my second trip to India was far more eventful than the first, I still had little concrete evidence to verify we had made a change in the lives of many people. We had spent about a week in one remote village that had never heard the gospel. People responded to the messages and some even came through to water baptism before we left. A little girl with one leg 11/2 to 2 inches shorter than the other causing her to waddle from side-to-side was healed in front of everyone. Before we left the village I got very sick. By the time we got back to

New Delhi I was getting dehydrated and had to be hospitalized. I thought I was going to die.

Over the years I wondered what lasting affect we had on the people of that village. Ten or fifteen years later I received a newsletter from the organization we had worked with in that part of India. One of the articles showed a picture of the new church building that had been built in a village to replace the first building they had out grown. They were thanking people for giving the funds to expand the church. It was the village where we had preached and prayed and baptized and left.

Be encouraged. Don't give up doing right. You are having an impact—you just don't know it yet! May the Lord give you insight this week into the good you have already done.

Notes

[1] Ecclesiastes 11:1

Better Way 15: What You Need Is Already At Hand

*"The Lord said to him,
'What is that in your hand?'..."*[1]

January 25, 2011 at *ShizuDai* (Shizuoka University), I needed a paperclip to keep some documents together. I looked on the floor of the classroom but didn't see one. I just had this feeling a clip was there. Remembering my relationship with God and paperclips (see Better Way 6), Philippians 4:19 flashed through my mind. "My God shall supply all your needs according to his riches in glory in Christ Jesus." I saw two trash cans against the wall.

"Move the trash cans." Would the Holy Spirit say something like that? I moved the first can. Nothing. But, underneath the second can was one, very normal paperclip. This was a simple object lesson. What I needed was there all the time. I just couldn't see it. Two verses that have meant much to me the past few years came to mind. "It will also come to pass that before they call, I will answer; and while they are still speaking, I will hear."[2] "And I will give you the treasures of darkness and hidden riches of secret places, that you may know that it is I, the Lord, the God of Israel, Who calls you by your name."[3] A paperclip is not a great treasure, unless you need one!

God told Moses to cast his rod on the ground. When he did, "...it became a serpent [the symbol of royal and divine power worn on the crown of the Pharaohs]; and Moses fled from before it."[4] Moses had been a shepherd for 40 years. He had possibly had this same rod for many of those years. He had no idea that the rod he had leaned on, that he had used to walk countless miles in the wilderness, and that he had kept beside him when he slept could become a serpent. Lance Lambert said that the Hebrew word used for "serpent" here is the same word used for sand viper, the most venomous snake in the Sinai desert. No wonder Moses fled from it! He not only didn't have his trusty rod to kill the viper, his rod now WAS the viper. Yet, that simple rod would become Moses' first weapon to assault the demonic forces behind the throne of Egypt. His first miracle was a direct confrontation with the crown of Pharaoh. God told him "...take this rod in your hand with which you shall work the signs [that prove I sent you]."[5] That inanimate piece of wood would become his instrument for working miracles! It had been with him for years but, now, with God's empowering, it would be used to set a nation free.

We can get discouraged when we have a need but don't see anything or any way to take care of it. We look at our bankbook, our lack of education, or all our other limited resources and feel hopeless. Don't give up, don't give in, and don't run away. Be encouraged. The better way is to think, "What I need is already at hand. Help me see it, Lord."

More

The owner of a scrap metal business wanted to support missions and Christian work but didn't have the money. He saw the needs and had the desire, but didn't know how he could contribute. In prayer he thought of a purchase he had made that didn't seem to yield any return. He had a huge supply of large, WWII batteries now sitting on his lot. They were stacked about 2 stories high and 2 football fields long. They were not your normal car batteries but he didn't really know what their intended use had been. Cutting one open he was surprised to find a significant amount of silver inside. Further research revealed they were a type of silver oxide battery the Germans were developing for use in tanks, torpedoes, or other vehicles and weapons. The amount of silver in his vast supply yielded a very sizable financial return on his initial investment. He generously gave to support the Lord's work.

What he needed was sitting right there in front of him. He just needed the eyes of the Lord to see what was at hand.

Notes

[1] Exodus 4:2
[2] Isaiah 65:24
[3] Isaiah 45:3 Amplified Bible
[4] Exodus 4:3 Amplified Bible
[5] Exodus 4:17 Amplified Bible

Better Way 16: Be Still and Let God Sort Out *As & When* He Wills

*"O God... we are powerless before this
great multitude who are coming
against us;
nor do we know what to do, but our
eyes are on You."*[1]

Some years ago I was traveling by car and listening to a PBS radio program. A leading authority on longevity was speaking to the Washington Press Club. When asked, "What is the single most important thing we can do to increase our life span?" the speaker replied, "Choose your parents wisely." In other words, the most important thing you can do to insure a long life was out of your control before you were even conceived! We have to realize that there are just certain things that have affected and will affect us that we can't do anything about.

I keep the key to our church on a round key chain that is engraved with St. Francis of Assisi's Serenity prayer. Having spent several years in a Faith/Word church, I used to see this prayer as one people prayed when they lacked faith. After all, can't we change anything and everything that comes our way if we just have a scripture to believe, confess, and unwaveringly cleave unto? After being in leadership in America for about 8 years and pastoring an international, multi-racial church in Japan for the past 25 years, I have come to appreciate the wisdom of this brief request of the Lord. "God grant me the serenity to accept the things I cannot change, courage to change the things I can, and the wisdom to know the difference." There are people and situations that are just out of my control. I can waste time being stressed over these or I can just leave them to the Lord to sort out *as* and *when* He wills.

When I was in graduate school at Auburn University, we studied St. Augustine's writings on rhetoric and homiletics. Augustine was a brilliant man and professor of rhetoric before his conversion. He had a reputation as an eloquent orator before delivering his first sermon. After becoming the archbishop of Hippo in northern Africa, people came from neighboring cities and even other countries to hear him preach. One Sunday, shortly after he had started his sermon, a woman in the back of the church started to shout. When people recognized her and learned what had just happened, they, too, started to shout. The commotion spread throughout the church to the point that Augustine could no longer be heard.

The woman was a well known blind lady who sat daily in the street asking alms of all who came near. At the beginning of his sermon, the lady's eyes were opened and she was blind no more. She could not contain her excitement and neither could those around her. The shouting increased as news of her miracle spread throughout the congregation. Augustine quietly sat down as the joyful celebrants spilled into the streets to proclaim God's goodness.

Some of Augustine's youthful disciples were incensed that the people had been so disrespectful of their master. One asked Augustine, "Why didn't you tell them to be quiet and sit down? Some people traveled a great distance to hear you preach today."

Augustine simply replied, "The Lord was preaching so much more eloquently than I, I needed to be quiet and sit down."

We know earthquakes, tornados, and tsunamis are out of our control yet we are so shocked when people and situations don't change no matter what we do. Sometimes, like king Jehoshaphat, we just have to cry out, "O God, we are powerless and we don't know what to do, but our eyes are on You!"[2] We need to recognize when God is preaching—whether through words or signs—humble ourselves, and sit quietly while He works. After all, whatever He does or says is far more eloquent than anything we can attempt.

Notes

[1] 2 Chronicles 20:12
[2] *Ibid.*

Better Way 17: Choose What You Ponder

"Don't go home for Christmas. You'll never make it to New Year's without giving birth!" our doctor warned. So my wife and I were practicing our breathing exercises in eager anticipation of a Christmas or New Year's delivery! Sarah was finally induced and gave birth to Christopher David on January 19th!

I particularly remember the natural childbirth instructor telling us to take an object to the hospital for Sarah to concentrate on while breathing. By focusing on the object and breathing correctly she would not be able to concentrate on the pain of the contractions as they increased in intensity and duration. The idea is that we, as humans, cannot concentrate on two or more things at the same time. If we concentrate on one task or event, we will be distracted from focusing on another. So, if we practice focusing on a positive task, person, or event, before a more painful task, person, or event enters our life, we will be able to overcome and succeed. [I realize that never having experienced childbirth myself I cannot really give an accurate testimony regarding the efficacy of concentrating on an object and breathing so you don't notice the pains of a new life trying to burst into our world. However this is what we were taught and it must at least help or these people would not continue to be employed.]

Each year we celebrate the birth of Jesus Christ. Before and during this event Mary experienced intense and, probably, conflicting emotions. She was found to be with child before her legal marriage and had risked public humiliation and stoning. She gave birth in a strange town in less than ideal surroundings without the benefit of her mother and father. Add to this the promises of Gabriel and then the story of the angels singing in the fields. Her final response is summed up by Luke, "But Mary treasured all these things, pondering them in her heart."[1] The NLT says she, "...thought about them often." Mary made a choice what she was going to dwell on—again and again. During the flight to Egypt, eventual return to Nazareth, and over the next 30 years she "treasured" and "pondered" on the incredible promises about her son.

After providing a list of good, positive things, Paul encourages the believers at Philippi to "...think on and weigh and take account of these things [fix your minds on them]."[2] We can reduce the stress we experience by fixing our minds on the good things God has given us. In the next verse Paul says, "Practice what you have learned."[3] Practice before difficult things happen and then keep on practicing as you go through. Hopefully you won't have to keep treasuring and pondering for thirty years like Mary. But, on the other hand, once her son revealed His glory by turning water into wine, it was one miracle and healing after another for the next 3 years!

Practice Pondering Providential Promises!

More

As we were preparing to celebrate the twenty-fourth anniversary of our church in Japan, a lady who had been with us for almost 20 years informed me by e-mail that she was no longer mentally or physically able to talk to anyone face-to-face or by telephone. She further informed me that she would not be coming to our house to help as she had one day a week for the past fifteen years. Furthermore, she could not come to church either. A few days later she wrote to say that when she recovered she would start over again at another church. The next day she wrote to say her decision was firm and she would definitely not return to our church or home. She made it clear she would not talk to us about this to explain or be helped. These e-mails cast a dark shadow over my thoughts to celebrate the church's anniversary.

I had a choice to make. Do I ponder the actions of one person and the others who have left over the years or do I ponder the far greater good we have accomplished in the lives of so many? It is amazing how one act of betrayal can outweigh so many loyal and faithful actions of others. I have to consciously set my mind on the good things in order not to be overcome with the bad. When Paul wrote to the Romans, "Do not be overcome by evil but overcome evil with good,"[4] this must surely include our thought life as well as our actions. I must make my mind dwell on good things in order not to be overcome with evil things!

Our little church in Shizuoka has had an impact on the lives of people in many countries. Not only have we been instrumental in people receiving Jesus and being baptized here in our city but we now have people who have attended our church living in 18 countries around the world. We have touched people in 6 of the 7 continents [so far no one from Antarctica has attended our church]. One young couple who were with us for only 1 year became missionaries in Brazil for 5 years. A young lady who was only with us for 1 month later served as a missionary in Honduras and Haiti before returning to live in Australia. A young woman of Greek descent married an Algerian and journeyed with him to France as a missionary couple. A girl from Tehran married an Iranian man living in California and now works with his church in San Diego evangelizing political refugees from their homeland. An Indonesia girl returned to her country, got married, and started a church based on the life she experienced at Living Way. There are others scattered around the globe but I have no idea what wonderful things they are accomplishing!

The better way is to think on these things. It's a choice of will that pays valuable dividends.

Notes

[1] Luke 2:19
[2] Philippians 4:8 Amplified Bible
[3] Philippians 4:9
[4] Romans 12:21

Better Way 18: I'm Not Where I Want To Be BUT I'm Not Where I've Been

Medical Trivia: Every few years you have replaced the 50 to 70 trillion cells in your body (except for the neurons in your cerebral cortex). Some cells live for only a few days, others a few weeks, and a very few for 1 to 2 years. Our brain cells don't replace themselves but we only use about 10% at any given time anyway! So, literally, you are not the same person you were just a few years ago.

We may get discouraged when we think of the New Year and are pressed to make New Year's Resolutions. I could just pull out my same list from years past. This year I'm going to lose weight, exercise at least 3 times a week, AND go to bed early and get up early! I haven't been able to keep those resolutions consistently for very long! The Japanese have a saying for this—*mikkabouzu*. It refers to a person who can't stick to anything for over 3 days! I *have* done better than that.

No matter where you are, you have made progress! You are literally (physically) not the same person you were last year. In my 60 years I've renewed myself many times already—without even trying! Isn't our God an amazing designer?! Paul revealed his motivation to the believers at Philippi and to us.

"...I press on so that I may lay hold of that for which also I was laid hold of by Christ Jesus... one thing I do: forgetting what lies behind and reaching forward to what lies ahead, I press on toward the goal for the prize..."[1]

Twice he encouraged us to "press on." Don't get complacent or discouraged and quit. Proverbs 1:32 warns, "...the complacency of fools will destroy them." The Amplified Bible is even more blunt when it translates the original script as "the careless ease of [self-confident] fools shall destroy them." Sarah and I lived in Decatur, AL for ten years before we came to Japan. Almost every day I read this quote by Admiral Stephen Decatur at the top of The Decatur Daily Newspaper, "There is no hope for the satisfied man." I guess it permanently imprinted itself on my long term memory.

Then Paul says, "forgetting what lies behind." It is much easier to press on if you forget what has already happened. "Forgetting" can be translated, literally as "to lose out of mind," or "neglecting." It is okay to neglect those bad memories. Don't keep visiting past mistakes and failures. Press on toward the goal. Keep looking ahead to the prize.

Be encouraged. Start the New Year by repeating to yourself, "I'm Not Where I Want To Be BUT I'm Not Where I've Been!" That's a better way.

Notes

[1] Philippians 3:12-14

Better Way 19: Plan How To Respond Ahead Of Time

I recently read an article about "proactive coping." Most coping strategies focus on reacting to stressful situations we are already experiencing. A proactive approach means we plan how we will respond to certain events. Don't sit around fantasizing how you will react if someone dies or if your business goes bankrupt. This in itself would be a negative (and potentially stressful) approach. However, when you know that you will be entering a stress producing situation, confrontation, time of the year, meeting with your boss, or going to a family reunion where your cantankerous Uncle Harry will be waiting, prepare positive responses and Godly alternatives.

For example, if you know from past experience that a certain person loves to stir up controversy and provoke strife, plan ahead (1) not to take the bait and (2) how to defuse the bomb he lights in others. Proverbs 15:1 (The Message) says, "A gentle response defuses anger, but a sharp tongue kindles a temper-fire." Too many times I only think of the "gentle response" hours or days after I am out of the situation. We need to pray into the situation before it happens. The Boy Scout motto is "Be Prepared." Peter, who knew all too well what NOT to say and do when caught off guard, tells us "always *being* ready to make a defense to everyone who asks you to give an account for the hope that is in you, yet with gentleness and reverence."[1] With his temperament he had learned he better be prepared not only with the answer but also with the proper attitude—with gentleness and reverence! No more whacking off servant's ears or cursing at little girls.

Being proactive involves thinking and praying ahead. Paul told the Ephesians to, "Look carefully then how you walk! Live purposefully and worthily and accurately, not as the unwise and witless, but as wise (sensible, intelligent people), making the very most of the time [buying up each opportunity], because the days are evil. Therefore do not be vague and thoughtless and foolish, but understanding and firmly grasping what the will of the Lord is."[2] In order to make the most of every opportunity we have to think and understand. The foolish are those who go through life without ever thinking about what they are doing, either before they do something or after they have finished! Proactive coping—being prepared before you enter a lions' den—will reduce the stress both in the situation and later!

Notes

[1] 1 Peter 3:15
[2] Ephesians 5:15-17 Amplified Bible

Better Way 20: Learn To Overlook Some Things

"A man's discretion makes him slow to anger, and it is his glory to overlook a transgression."[1]

"Overlook" in this passage means "to pass over, to pass through, to pass by, or to pass on."[2] "Transgression" can be translated as "a breach of trust; a rebellious act;[3] or, "an offense."[4] So King Solomon, a man of incredible wisdom who wielded almost absolute power over his subjects, declares it is a man's glory to pass by and go on through the offenses of others. There are things people say and do that we need to just overlook and keep going. The Message says, just "forgive and forget."

A few weeks before we left America I met with a man who was very angry with me. He refused to be reconciled no matter what I said. As we parted, one of his last comments was, "God will never let you leave this city!" Well, we did leave. Six months after settling in Japan, I received a letter from him declaring, "You will never succeed on the mission field. You will fail!"

I never wrote him back. We just kept going. This year, 2013, we celebrated our 28th year as missionaries.

When King David was fleeing the rebellion of his son Absalom, Shimei, a relative of King Saul, was following on a ridge above David shouting insults and throwing rocks. One of David's mighty men offered to remove Shimei's head to shut him up. David told the man, "Let him alone and let him curse... perhaps the Lord will look on my affliction and return good to me instead of his cursing this day."[5] In the end God did turn the cursing into blessing and David was restored to his kingdom. A short time after David's death, one of David's loyal men executed Shimei when he refused to obey the command of King Solomon.

In his book, *Every Day a Friday*, Joel Osteen quotes a study on friendship. "Researchers found that 25% of the people you meet will not like you. The next 25% won't like you but could be persuaded to. Another 25% will like you but could be persuaded not to, and the final 25% will like you and stand by you no matter what." He concludes by saying, "If you take those statistics to heart, you should feel free of any acceptance anxiety. Just realize that some people won't like you no matter what you do, so don't waste your time and energy trying to win them over."[6] That 25% who will never like you will probably say and do things you will be well advised to overlook. Reduce the stress in your life by just passing on by the insults, curses, and flying rocks. Keep your head low and move on. Heed David's wisdom, "Leave him alone and let him curse." In the end, God will hear and turn the cursing into blessing! We've enjoyed 28 years of blessing in Japan and expect a lot more.

"What people in the world think of
you is really none of your business."
Martha Graham

Notes

[1] Proverbs 19:11
[2] Strong's Concordance, *abar*, h5674a
[3] Strong's Concordance, *pesha*, h6588
[4] Amplified Bible includes this translations
[5] 2 Samuel 16:11-12; see Deuteronomy 23:5 + Romans 8:28
[6] Joel Osteen, *Everyday A Friday*, p. 218, iBook

Better Way 21: Make the Choice to Bend Rather Than Break

A few days before departing for my very first mission trip to India in 1980, a lady in our church told me, "I don't know what this means but I feel the Lord is saying, 'From this moment *time has no meaning*.'" I didn't understand either until I had spent a few days in India where the statement, "I'll pick you up at 9:00 really means anywhere from nine to eleven." I learned that not only time but all schedules and plans are subject to constant revision and/or cancellation at a moment's notice.

Now, 32 years later, as my first mission trip to Indonesia is ending, I know more than ever the necessity to be flexible. Before we left Japan we had planned to have a Relationship Seminar at the oldest Assembly of God church in Kalimantan that would have several other churches participating. Ando, my son-in-law, and I would both teach a session and have Hannah, my daughter, share some of her testimony, too. We thought we would have at least 2 hours to speak and that an interpreter would be provided for us. When we arrived at the church we were told the meeting was from 7:00 to 9:00 P.M. but that it had not been advertised as a Relationship Seminar. Actually, we were speaking at the regular Sunday night church meeting. We would have worship for about 45 minutes and then only one of us would have time to share. In addition, the person who was to interpret was sick so Ando would have to translate. Everything changed but we only found out when we arrived. There was nothing we could do but adapt to the situation.

Psalms 37:4 says, "Delight yourself in the Lord; and he shall give you the desires of your heart." "Delight" means "to be soft or pliable, delicate, dainty."[1] Pliable means to be "flexible and easily bent or molded." If you translate this verse, "Be pliable in the Lord..." you get the idea that in order for the Lord to give me the desires of my heart I must be flexible in His hands. If I am soft then He can bend me and mold me any way He wishes. If I am hard, I will not bend but break.

When I was at university, a friend once told me, "I always get what I want from the Lord because I know what to want." He explained that if he was willing to adapt to the Lord's desires and make them *his* desires then he always got what he desired. Make the choice to bend rather than break. Be soft, be flexible in the Lord. That will significantly reduce the stress in any one's life.

Notes

[1] Strong's Concordance, h6026, *anog*

Better Way 22: Pray for Those Who Betray You

"But understand this, that in the last days will come (set in) perilous times of great stress and trouble [hard to deal with and hard to bear]. For people will be lovers of self and [utterly] self-centered... [They will be] without natural [human] affection (callous and inhuman), relentless (admitting of no truce or appeasement)... treacherous [betrayers]... Avoid all such people [turn away from them]."[1]

Some years ago an older woman and her thirty-something year old daughter came to the front after a Sunday service, hugged me, and said, "You are the best Bible teacher we have ever heard. We love you and appreciate you so much." A few minutes later a middle-aged divorcee told me, "I really enjoy this church. This was the place I had been trying to find for years. This is so wonderful." That was the last time I saw any of these women. Later I learned they had joined other churches. I was totally caught off guard, hurt, and offended. I can look back *now* and appreciate what I learned. I didn't handle it so well then.

Paul warned Timothy, his son in the faith, about what was coming in the near future. "Perilous times of great stress and trouble that are hard to deal with and hard to bear"[2] are coming. Then he explains that this great stress and trouble will be caused by the character and actions of people. The stress that is most difficult to bear comes from those who are nearest to us.

Seven hundred years before Paul warned Timothy, David wrote about his own painful experience.

"For it is not an enemy who reproaches me, then I could bear it; nor is it one who hates me who has exalted himself against me, then I could hide myself from him. But it is you, a man my equal, my companion and my familiar friend; we who had sweet fellowship together, Walked in the house of God in the throng."[3]

David felt the pain of betrayal by his familiar friend—a fellow believer with whom he had worshipped and enjoyed sweet fellowship. This was much harder to deal with than the attack of an enemy.

Jesus "knew all men... and He Himself knew what was in man."[4] He knew they could shout "Hosanna" one day and "Crucify Him" the next. Jesus told us how to respond to the stress caused by being in relationship with other human beings.

"Invoke blessings upon and pray for the happiness of those who curse you, implore God's blessing (favor) upon those who abuse you [who revile, reproach, disparage, and high-handedly misuse you]."[5]

Why should I pray for the happiness of someone who has hurt me? Why should I implore God's blessing and favor on someone who mistreated me? Since God knows the hearts of all people and nothing is hidden from His sight, then He knows why people act so badly. He knows both cause and effect. I am experiencing the effect—being spitefully abused, rejected, betrayed, cursed, etc. However, I may not (and probably don't) know the unseen need driving that person. He does.

Jesus says, "Implore the Father to meet the need of the person hurting you." They treat you badly because they are unhappy. They speak evil of you and break relationship because they are not enjoying the favor and blessing of God. They are acting out of their own misery and struggles. Don't waste your time and energy nursing your hurt and endlessly repeating, "Why? Why? Why?" Pray the solution.

"Dear Father, please help this person find happiness. Bless them with your gracious and boundless favor. And, if there is the need, we trust that 'the kindness of God leads to repentance.'"[6] Repeat this prayer again and again if necessary. It never hurts us to pray, especially when we are praying for another's blessing and happiness. This is a far better way than calling down curses and staying wounded in your own soul and spirit.

Notes

1 2 Timothy 3:1-5 Amplified Bible
2 2 Timothy 3:1 Amplified Bible
3 Psalms 55:12-14
4 John 2:24-25
5 Luke 6:28 Amplified Bible
6 Romans 2:4

Better Way 23: Use That Big Stick in the Corner

"What's that big stick in the corner?" I asked my long time friend, Rajan, as I pointed at a 4 ft. (121 cm.) branch propped against the wall of his first floor living room.

"It's to kill scorpions and cobras," he said rather matter-of-factly.

Rajan and his family had pioneered a church in an uninhabited section of Madurai, Tamil Nadu (south India) called "Mosquito Mountain" by the locals. Mosquitos ruled the air but scorpions and cobras dominated the terrain. Rajan's church and house had so improved the property that now new roads had been cut and other houses were filling in the neighborhood. However, not all the original inhabitants had given up their claim to the land.

"A few nights ago," Rajan explained, "we were sitting on the floor having our night time prayers with the children. It was so hot we had to keep the doors and windows open. As we prayed a large scorpion came charging through the door into the middle of the room. Rose (his wife) grabbed the big stick and quickly killed it before the flailing tail could sting anyone." That big stick in the corner became a much more respected piece of furniture in my eyes.

"Oh, when you take a bath tonight, be sure the rock on the shower floor covers the drain hole when you are finished. It's to keep cobras from crawling into the house from the field," Rajan instructed as I prepared to head to the bath. Believe me, I didn't take my eyes off that rock while I was bathing. Let's get back to that big stick.

What come's charging into your life when you're trying to hear the Lord? Is it fear? Or, doubt? Or, just that feeling of being so overwhelmed you can't do even one more little thing. You better have a big stick in your corner to kill that critter from hell before you really get hurt!

When fear runs in, reach for "God hath not given us the spirit of fear but of power, and of love and of a sound mind."[1] If doubt has the audacity to cross your threshold, grab Mark 10:27, "...all things are possible with God." When that overwhelming scorpion makes you want to just give up and quit, don't run and hide. Retrieve your big stick and come out swinging—"I can do all things through Christ who strengthens me."[2] If you need an even bigger stick use the Amplified version, " I have strength for all things in Christ Who empowers me [I am ready for anything and equal to anything through Him Who infuses inner strength into me; I am self-sufficient in Christ's sufficiency]." God has a big stick for every demonic varmint.

Rajan knew what kind of animals were likely to enter his house and he was ready for them.

Likewise, we know the sins and weaknesses that most often attack us. The only offensive weapon to our spiritual armor is the "sword of the Spirit, which is the word (*rhema*) of God."[3] The *rhema* or "now word," is your big stick to keep ready in the corner! Have it ready and USE it!

Notes

[1] 2 Timothy 1:7 KJV
[2] Philippians 4:13 NKJV
[3] Ephesians 6:17

Better Way 24: Before I'm Surprised, He's Provided

"It will also come to pass that before
they call,
I will answer; and while they are still
speaking,
I will hear."[1]

"The check is in the mail," is a clichéd joke these days. The bill collector on the telephone rarely believes you really mailed the check *before* he called. But, this is exactly what God has done again and again. The answer is on the way even before we know we have a problem. Before I'm surprised, He's already provided.

After happily living in our three floor apartment in downtown Shizuoka city for almost ten years, our real estate agent informed us that our building had been sold to a person in Tokyo. We had six months to find a new place. The rental laws in Japan favor renters who have lived in a place for a long time so, to avoid any complications, the new owner offered us an unusual deal. If we would vacate the premises by December 31, he would give us the next six months rent free and promised to give back our two month's deposit. This would effectively give us eight months rent to put on a new place.

Although the money would definitely help, that was not our biggest problem. Ten years before, we had scoured the city to find any place big enough for our family at a price we could afford. Plus, local people were hesitant to rent to any foreigner, much less one who had 10 children! I was particularly dismayed by this problem. Rent is high in this city and houses are small. We looked everywhere. At one point we even considered renting two houses in the same neighborhood and splitting up the family.

Three months before the deadline the only place we could find was for sale—not for rent. We didn't have the $425,000 they were asking and we didn't know a bank that would make a loan to a foreigner. Besides, most banks here require about 25% of the total value as a down payment before they will loan the rest. My stress level went off the charts. I was overwhelmed and in shock by this unexpected turn of events. God was not. Before we called, He had already answered.

Other than the unusually generous offer of the new owner of our apartment, God had already orchestrated events, people, and situations to provide all we needed to buy the house. These included:

1. The new house had been on the market for one year so the company who bought it at auction was eager to sell and willing to negotiate.

2. We had been renting our church building from a man whose son worked at Shizuoka Bank so he knew all about us and we had established a good reputation with his family. (A few years later the banker left the bank.)

3. Shizuoka Bank was pushing people to make house loans.

4. A friend opened the door at an American conference for me to share and raise money and others were generous to give.

Sarah and I dropped off the key to our old apartment just before midnight December 31, 2004 and joined the family for New Year's in our new home.

When you're surprised, look for God's advance provision. Before you know you have a question, He has the answer. Before you even see the problem, He's got the solution. The check *really is* in the mail.

More

"Chris, we have guests coming for lunch in a few minutes. I need you to run to the little store and buy two loaves of bread."

"No problem, Dad," replied my reliable little eight year old.

"All I have is this ¥10,000 bill so you need to be very careful. Put it deep in your pocket and don't touch it until you have to pay. Then carefully put the change in your pocket and come straight home."

Chris assured me I could trust him and I did. He was always careful, especially about money. We lived in a small, very country community between a large city to the west across the river and a medium sized one to the east. The store was very near and everyone in the neighborhood knew our children so I wasn't worried about his safety. (Please note this was 1989 and even America, especially Alabama, was relatively safe back then.)

We were hurriedly cleaning and straightening for our guests to arrive when the telephone rang. I could tell my wife was talking to Chris. Before she handed me the phone she warned, "Stay calm. Chris is upset and afraid to talk to you."

"Dad, I can't find the ¥10,000 bill any where. The people at the store helped me look all up and down the aisles but we can't find it."

I reassured Chris it was alright and I would be there soon. I knew the path he always took to the store so I kept sweeping my eyes back and forth as I weaved my way to the little neighborhood grocery. I didn't see anything. Together Chris and I vainly searched the store. Then we slowly walked back to the house praying and looking. Nothing.

That evening I was walking home from my English class I taught at a small cram school about three blocks from the house. My mind drifted to a conversation Chris and I had a few days before. A lady in our old neighborhood had hired Chris to help teach her children's English class every Saturday. She paid him a few hundred yen to play with the other kids in English.

"Chris, you're making money now," I said. "You know you need to tithe from your income."

He admitted he hadn't thought about that. We talked about the meaning of tithing and Chris promised he would pay his tithe the next day. Sunday night he told me he not only put in his 10% but gave a little extra to make up for the times he had forgotten.

Remembering this conversation disturbed my spirit and I knew we had to do something. When I got home I went straight upstairs to Chris' sleeping area and reminded him of our conversation. Then I read Malachi 3:10-11 to him.

Bring the whole tithe into the storehouse, so that there may be food in My house, and test Me now in this," says the Lord of hosts, "if I will not open for you the windows of heaven and pour out for you a blessing until it overflows. Then I will rebuke the devourer for you..."

I said, "Chris, this just isn't right. Sunday you paid your tithes. You did what the Bible said but on Monday the devourer came in and stole ¥10,000 from you. That's not right, is it?"

"No, I don't think it is," he agreed.

"Okay, then, we are going to stand on the Word and ask God to rebuke the devourer and command him to give back what he stole." We agreed in prayer and stood on the truth of the Word together. That was Monday night.

Wednesday afternoon we had our weekly Bible study with a few ladies from our church. When they left, I saw an envelope on the kitchen table. "Sarah, what's this?"

"I don't know. Kuni-san laid it down as she was walking out."

There was nothing written on the envelope and no note—just two ¥10,000 bills inside. I was stunned. I immediately called Kuni-san and asked what this money was for and why she had left it.

She said, "It was the strangest thing. Monday morning I was ironing and I suddenly had this great heaviness come over me. I didn't know what to do so I just stopped and prayed. I ran out of words to pray in Japanese so I started praying in tongues. Then I had this impression, 'Give Ricky Gordon some money.' I didn't know how much to give so I hope it was enough." Then she added, "I'm sorry I waited until today but I knew I was coming to your house on Wednesday for the Bible study."

I quickly explained the miracle in which she was such a key participant and ran upstairs to find Chris. "God's Word is true, Chris! Look at this," I said as I pulled out the two crisp bills. I've never forgotten my eight year old son's next words.

"Dad, now I know God is real because he answered *MY* prayers."

When we were looking for the lost bill, God was speaking to a lady on the other side of town. Before we read the scriptures and prayed according to God's promises, the Holy Spirit had already directed someone to pay back what the devourer had taken. God's Word is always true and He never forgets a promise!

Notes

[1] Isaiah 65:24

Better Way 25: Stay Focused

Ericah (my 4th daughter) was trying to teach English to 10 rambunctious three to five year old children while three mothers were observing to decide if they wanted their little progeny to join the class. In an effort to gain some control over the activity she announced they would play a game. Gathering her little chicks in front of her like a mother hen she explained the rules. She would call out a color in English and the class would have to repeat the name of the color. Then they were to scurry around the room until they found the color and tell the teacher. Ericah held up a card with a primary color and proclaimed loudly, "Red!"

Everyone shouted back, "Red!" then scattered to locate the color.

"Teacher, I found 'Red,'" announced darling little Sho, holding out his hand. His hand was covered in red—red blood. His nose was bleeding.

Almost without thinking, Ericah wiped his hand, picked up Sho, placed a tissue in his nose to stop the bleeding, and continued with the game—still holding Sho in her arms. She had a lesson to complete in forty-five minutes and prospective mothers watching. The owner of the school, who was also watching, was very impressed with Ericah's calm demeanor.

Ericah is a wonderful example of making a better choice. She could have screamed or panicked at the sight of blood or frightened the child and the other children by making too big a fuss. Instead, she took care of the immediate issue and stayed focused on the task at hand.

Both Mark and Luke tell the story of Jairus imploring Jesus to come quickly to his house and heal his twelve year old daughter before she dies. Jesus' journey is interrupted when a woman suffering from a hemorrhage for the past twelve years touches the hem of his garment. Immediately, Jesus perceiving that power had flowed from him stopped to identify the woman who had drawn healing from that touch. While Jesus confirms her healing, a messenger arrives saying, "...Your daughter has died. Why bother the Teacher any further?" Then, Mark, writes, "Overhearing[1] but ignoring what they said, Jesus said to the ruler of the synagogue, Do not be seized with alarm and struck with fear; only keep on believing."[2] Jesus heard the report but chose to "ignore what they said." He stayed focused on the goal. He encouraged the father to "keep on believing" as they continued their journey to the house. At Jairus' home he was openly mocked for proclaiming the little girl was not really dead. Putting his mockers outside, he completed his mission with two words, "Talitha cumi!"[3]

Jesus made the choice to continue believing what His father had told him to do and not be distracted from finishing the task at hand. He stayed focused on his mission. When we allow ourselves to get sidetracked, especially by negative reports, our stress level dramatically escalates. We may change direction or just give up completely. A better way is to "take no heed" to the "nattering nabobs of negativism"[4] and don't join their "4-H Club—the hopeless, hysterical hypochondriacs of history."[5] Stay focused. Press on to complete the goal.

Notes

[1] Strong's Concordance, "overhearing" *parakouo*, g3878, means "to overhear, to hear amiss, to take no heed"
[2] Mark 5:35-36 Amplified Bible
[3] Mark 5:41 Amplified Bible
[4] According to the Congressional Record, this term was first used during Agnew's address to the California Republican state convention in San Diego on September 11, 1970. In context, it was used together with another well-known Agnew alliteration: "In the United States today, we have more than our share of the nattering nabobs of negativism. They have formed their own 4-H Club—the "hopeless, hysterical hypochondriacs of history."
[5] *Ibid.*

Better Way 26: Let Your Advocate Handle It

*"...the accuser of our brethren is cast
down, which accused them before our
God day and night."[1]*

*"...we have an advocate who pleads
our case before the Father. He is Jesus
Christ,
the one who is truly righteous."[2]*

Shortly after I published my first book I received an e-mail from someone in another country requesting a free copy of the book. They explained they had heard about me from another foreigner and wanted to read my book but had limited funds. I gladly sent a free copy and paid the airmail postage myself. A few months later I received another e-mail from this person who said they had worked as a journalist before going taking up their current post. Then they added, "There were so many grammatical mistakes in your book I almost couldn't finish reading it."

I was shocked at first but then offended by the comments. I've been teaching English and Speech for over thirty years. I even teach an English composition class at the university. I had probably read my book at least four times looking for errors. Three close friends had read the book and made comments and corrections plus my publisher had gone over the manuscript. My pride was definitely aroused. Besides, how dare this ex-journalist ask for and receive a free copy and then make such a statement.

Once I got over my wounded ego, and knowing that having my pride exposed was for my own good, I contemplated how best to respond. I felt that just ignoring the letter would be too passive and, besides, I needed to acknowledge valid criticism. So, I wrote back thanking them for their remarks and said, "I may be printing a second edition in the future and don't want to make the same mistakes again. Would you please send me a list of all the grammatical mistakes you found so that I can correct them before the next printing?" It has been seven years and I am still waiting for that list.

In the Revelation of Jesus to John we learn there will come a time when "...the accuser of our brethren is cast down, which accused them before our God day and night." The devil's personal ministry is to accuse us before the Father. John tells us that we are never left at the mercy of this most persistent of all prosecutors. "We have an advocate who pleads our case before the Father. He is Jesus Christ, the one who is truly righteous."

The burden of proof belongs to the accuser. Don't let your pride prevent you from receiving and making necessary improvements but don't waste your time trying to find flaws you've never seen. If your critic has legitimate evidence, let him produce it. Otherwise, let your lawyer handle it.

Notes

[1] Revelations 12:10
[2] I John 2:1 NLT

Better Way 27: Never Quit in Defeat

When I made my first mission trip to India I had great expectations. Although I was only going to be there for 12 days, I envisioned healings, miracles, and hundreds rushing to the altar to give their lives to Jesus. Talking to a friend before we left, he said, "I hear it is so easy to evangelize in India you could stand up and just read the names out of a telephone book and people would get saved!" Such was my expectation. But, that was definitely not my experience.

Upon my return I had this conversation.

"How many people got saved in your meetings?"

"None that I know of."

"Well, how many people were healed?"

"We prayed for a lot of people but if they got healed they didn't tell me."

And, someone actually asked, "How many did you raise from the dead?" to which I replied, "I didn't even see any dead people!" I felt like a total failure.

I could almost hear them thinking, "You mean you spent $5,000 and 12 days in a foreign country and nothing happened?! Do the math. $5,000 divided by

'0' equals a bad investment. What a dud! You are clearly not missionary material!"

When I first returned, I completely agreed with them. But, at some time in my life, someone I don't remember told me, "Never quit in defeat." Someone taught me, "If at all possible, persevere until you attain some measure of victory. Then you can quit." I knew that if I never made another mission trip this would always be an area of defeat in my life. I had to go again. I determined to make one more trip to India. I felt like Jonathan when he invited his armor bearer to join him in attacking the Philistines. Basically he said, "Let's go. Who knows what God might do?!"[1] Jonathan wasn't moving in great confidence and faith but he felt like he had to try. The two men went, God routed the enemy, and Israel rallied.

My second trip was radically different from the first. People were saved, at least one person was visibly healed in the presence of many, and a new church was planted in virgin soil. And, I met and worked with Indian brothers on that trip that I am still working with today, over 30 years later.

When you feel you've failed, don't stop there. Make the choice to keep trying until you have at least some measure of success. Then you can quit (or change direction).

*"There is no failure except in
no longer trying."*[2]

Notes

[1] 1 Samuel 14:6 paraphrased by author
[2] Kin Hubbard and Elbert Hubbard

Better Way 28: Reject the Voice of Fear

One Sunday morning I was sharing about some experiences we've had in the church with spontaneous moves of the Holy Spirit. A split second before I shared one incident, a thought flashed through my mind, "I can't tell that story. Martin is here today. I know he doesn't believe in what I'm about to say." I judged that was a fear response and shared anyway.

I told about the Sunday people were lined up for prayer at the end of the service. Atsumi, who was at the back of the line, suddenly became weak in the knees and fell on the floor. Without anyone touching her, and much to her surprise, she began speaking words she had never learned nor heard. My son, Chris, knelt beside her to make certain she was unharmed. After a few minutes she asked him in Japanese, "What was I speaking?" Chris simply said, "You were speaking in tongues." She had never done that before and wasn't really sure what he was talking about.

After sharing the testimony I continued with my message and closed the meeting. That afternoon I spent an hour with a Christian lady who had attended our church for the first time. As she talked about difficulties she was having in her church and with the leadership, she commented, "I was really surprised that you talked about what happened to that girl in church. Our pastor never talks about anything like that in public." Part of her problem with the pastor was that he wouldn't discuss those issues in private either. To her it was important to know she could ask questions and that someone would listen and attempt to answer.

I was so glad I overcame my fear of what one person thought and spoke what I felt the Holy Spirit was leading me to share. Too often I have given in to that split second fear thought and altered my speech and actions. I knew the first thought was from the Holy Spirit. It was almost immediately countered by "You better not say that. You'll upset Martin!" I had a choice to make—which voice do I obey.

I don't always know if I am hearing the Holy Spirit, but, I almost always recognize the voice of fear. Regrettably, I've heard it a lot more and I *do* know *who* uses that voice. Fear is not from God. "God hath not given us a spirit of fear..."[1] "God is love"[2] and "perfect love casts out fear."[3] I am confident fear is not from God so when I recognize the voice of fear I make a choice. The better choice is reject fear every time!

Notes

[1] 2 Timothy 1:7 KJV
[2] 1 John 4:8
[3] 1 John 4:18

Better Way 29: Build Memorials Only To Victories

As a young boy I remember dreading one particular day of the year. As December 1 approached my mother would become increasingly gloomy. On that first day of December, for many years, we could feel her depression and frequently saw her weeping. We didn't talk about it much. We just knew that was the day my father, Sidney, was killed. My mother had memorialized his death by setting aside that one day a year to mourn.

Many of the feasts ordained by God for the people of Israel were to remember and celebrate victories over their enemies, e.g., Passover.[1] Joshua was told to place Memorial stones on the floor bed of the Jordan River and on the shore as Memorial Stones to remember their entering the Promised Land.[2] To my knowledge they were never told to build memorials to defeats or failures. We shouldn't do it either. Don't memorialize negative events.

I do believe the enemy of our souls tries to steal the memories of special events wrought by the hand of God and replace them with his. We have to consciously focus on the good God has done which means we have to intentionally look away from the bad Satan has done.

Philippians 4:8 in the Amplified Bible says, "For the rest, brethren, whatever is true, whatever is worthy of reverence *and* is honorable *and* seemly, whatever is just, whatever is pure, whatever is lovely *and* lovable, whatever is kind *and* winsome *and* gracious, if there is any virtue *and* excellence, if there is anything worthy of praise, think on *and* weigh *and* take account of these things [fix your minds on them]." In Hebrews 12: 2 in the Amplified Bible we are told, "Looking away [from all that will distract] to Jesus..." We have to intentionally focus on Jesus and the good things that have happened to us.

I was writing this section between classes at the university. Driving home I turned on a sermon by Joel Osteen titled "Remembering The Good." He just happened to say, "I remember December 1, 2003 when Mayer Lee Brown gave us the key to this beautiful facility. This building is a memorial stone. I still thank God for it." Immediately I knew I should replace the memorial stone to my father's death on December 1 with another. I can rejoice with the congregation of Lakewood Church that after a three year struggle they received the keys to their new building on December 1.

We make a choice when we build a memorial. Choose to build memorials only to victories. Replace any memorials to defeats with new ones!

"I recall all you have done, O Lord; I remember your wonderful deeds of long ago.
They are constantly in my thoughts. I cannot stop thinking about your mighty works."[3]

Notes

[1] Exodus 12
[2] Joshua 4
[3] Psalm 77:11-12 NLT

Better Way 30: Reconcile Your Head and Heart

"The longest journey in life is from your head to your heart."[1]

At 2:55 A.M. I was shocked awake by an internal tremor of intense emotion. "I spent three years convincing Rin that she could trust me... that I would take care of her... that she would always be safe with me. Then I gave her to a new family and stepped out of her life forever." A horrible sense of guilt almost forced the air out of my lungs. The feeling that I had betrayed a totally innocent, completely trusting little girl who had shown me nothing but unconditional love was overwhelming. I felt empty inside—so helpless. How would she ever understand? These emotions erupted from my subconscious. I was fully awake now!

Sitting alone in the dark, staring at a blue digital readout on the alarm clock, my reason kicked in and I once again assured myself that we made the right decision to place little Rin with a family that could care for her long after we had left *everyone* behind. As a healthy Down Syndrome child she will easily outlive us twenty or thirty years. We made the right decision—the best decision. Such head knowledge did not re-inflate the empty space in the center of my chest. What I knew in my head was not yet reconciled with what I felt in my heart.

"Just follow your heart and you'll never go wrong," says everyone from Richard Castle to Steve Jobs. Napoleon Dynamite agrees, "Just follow your heart. That's what I do." This doesn't quite fit with God's warning through Jeremiah that "The heart is deceitful above all things, and it is exceedingly perverse *and* corrupt and severely, mortally sick! Who can know it?"[2] If I had followed my heart, Rin would still be with us instead of with a loving family committed to her life-long care. I wouldn't be jarred awake with feelings of guilt and remorse. There *would* come a time though when I would have to face my own mortality. Then I would probably not even be able *to get to sleep* as I worried about who could provide for her when we were gone.

The cognitive dissonance experienced when heart and head disagree produces enough stress to seriously disrupt the sleep God promises His beloved ones. We need to apply "the Word that God speaks [which] is alive and full of power... sharper than any two-edged sword, penetrating to the dividing line of the breath of life (soul) and [the immortal] spirit, and of joints and marrow [of the deepest parts of our nature], exposing *and* sifting *and* analyzing *and* judging the very thoughts and purposes of the heart."[3] The Word is able to evaluate and determine the superior way—the way of the head or the way of the heart—for each person and situation. For there are times we need to follow the heart (particularly the redeemed heart). Other times it is best to follow the way of reason. The

Holy Spirit, applying the Word, is able to identify God's Way. David cried out, "...Give me understanding according to Your word."[4]

Jesus had a ministry of reconciliation—first and foremost reconciling us to God. He promised If we came to Him and learned from Him we would find rest for our souls. He is able to reconcile my head and my heart, too! So how will He reconcile *my* head and heart about this little girl?

God is a "father to the fatherless"[5] and He "sets the solitary in families."[6] Which family though? Rin could have died several times in her short 3 years, but she didn't. During that period of uncertainty, our family was the best family for her. Now, her future is much more certain. With an increased life expectancy of 50 to 60 years, another family has become the best one.

"To every thing there is a season, and a time to every purpose under the heaven."[7] In my head, I've moved on to the next season. My heart doesn't want to leave that season. I can't stay in that season of my life any more than I can make spring last all year long. Love draws a child near and makes her feel safe and secure. But then love, God's love, will release that child into a new place of safety and security. My heart *will* catch up with my head. As it does, the stress will decrease.

A BETTER WAY: MAKING BETTER CHOICES

*"The greatest distance in the universe
is the 14 inches from your head
to your heart."*

Notes

[1] Archbishop Donald Coven
[2] Jeremiah 17:9 Amplified Bible
[3] Hebrews 4:12 Amplified Bible
[4] Psalms 119:169
[5] Psalms 68:5 NLT
[6] Psalms 68:6 NKJV
[7] Ecclesiastes 3:1 KJV

What Jesus Knew: Keys to Successful Relationships

By Ricky Thomas Gordon

Why are we so surprised at what people say and do? Why are we so easily hurt and disappointed by people we love and trust? Because we do not know *What Jesus Knew*. When we know *What Jesus Knew* we will not be so easily shocked and discouraged by the actions of others.

In *What Jesus Knew* Ricky Gordon condenses the teachings of scripture into Thirty Principles that will make you wiser in relating to others both inside and outside the Body of Christ. The sound Biblical teaching illustrated with many personal experiences will improve your existing relationships and facilitate healing and restoration to broken ones.

Book is available at:
To His Glory Publishing Company,
Inc.
111 Sunnydale Court
Lawrenceville, GA 30044
(770) 458-7947
www.tohisglorypublishing.com

and
Amazon.com